RESTLESS PLANET

FLOODS

Emma Durham and Mark Maslin

WAYLAND

RESTLESS PLANET

FLOODS

Other titles in this series:

EARTHQUAKES STORMS VOLCANOES

Cover photograph: Garment factory workers returning home after work. They have to wade knee-deep through the flooded streets of Badda in Dhaka, Bangladesh in 1998.

Title page: People wading through the floodwaters that covered Honduras, Central America in 1998.

Contents page: Snowmelt floods in the Netherlands, caused by a warm spring following a cold winter.

First published in 1999 by Wayland Publishers Ltd,
61 Western Road, Hove, East Sussex, BN3 1JD, England
www.wayland.co.uk

This paperback edition published in 2000.

© Copyright 1999 Wayland Publishers Limited

Consultant: Bill Clarke, Education Officer, The Natural History Museum
Book editor: Hazel Songhurst
Series editor: Philippa Smith, Polly Goodman & Nicola Wright
Series design: Stonecastle Graphics
Book design: Tim Mayer

British Library Cataloguing in Publication Data
   Durham, Emma
   Floods. – (Restless Planet)
   1.Floods – Juvenile literature
   I.Title   II. Maslin, Mark
   551.4'89

ISBN 0 7502 2739 7

Printed and bound in Italy by G. Canale & C.S.p.A.

Acknowledgements
The publishers would like to thank the following for allowing their photographs to be reproduced in this book: Eye Ubiquitous 25, 39; GSF Picture Library 38; Oxford Scientific Films 6, 14, 15, 34, 45; Edward Parker 22, 30, 31; PHOTRI 10; Popperfoto *Title page*, *Contents page* 5, 16, 20, 26, 27, 28, 29, 44 (t); Science Photo Library 37, 44 (b); Still Pictures *Cover* (Shehzad Noorani), 4 (Jim Wark), 7 (Nigel Dickinson), 9 (Hjalte Tin),13 (Cyril Ruoso), 17 (RUBSAAT-UNEP), 23 (Heine Pedersen), 24 (William Campbell), 32 (Jorgen Schytte), 33 (Hjalted Tin), 34 (Norbert Wu), 41 (Nigel Dickinson), 42 (Gerard & Margi Moss).

Artwork by Nick Hawken and Tim Mayer

Contents

Introducing Floods

Floods happen when too much water overflows on to normally dry land, or when it collects in low-lying, poorly drained areas. Floods happen most often near rivers or close to the sea.

Flood-plains

The area of land next to a river or by the coast is called a flood-plain. Since flood-plains are often flat, fertile and close to water they have always been places where people have chosen to settle. In the USA, 10 million people live on flood-plains and a further 25 million live in areas which could be affected by flooding. However, by taking advantage of this land, people are also putting themselves at risk from the hazards of flooding.

▼ Flooded farmland on the flood-plain of the Mississippi River, USA.

▲ Boats carrying people through the flooded streets of Dhaka, the capital of Bangladesh, during the worst floods of the twentieth century.

In the news

Floods are so common that they are rarely out of the news, yet their impact is often underestimated. In February 1999, flooding was reported in Queensland, Australia, following heavy rain. At least four people lost their lives and several towns, businesses and houses were swamped. The town of Gympie, 150 km north of Brisbane, suffered its worst flooding in living memory. In July 1997, during severe flooding in the Czech Republic, Poland and Germany, flood barriers collapsed and thousands of people were evacuated. In total, 128 people died and the cost of the damage and the clean-up operation was estimated to be over $5 billion.

Worldwide floods

Hardly a week seems to pass without a flood occurring somewhere in the world. In 1998 in Bangladesh, over three-quarters of the country (an area larger than Austria) was flooded. Many of the floods reported in recent years have been described as the worst floods of the twentieth century. The causes have varied, ranging from the impact of a tsunami to torrential rain.

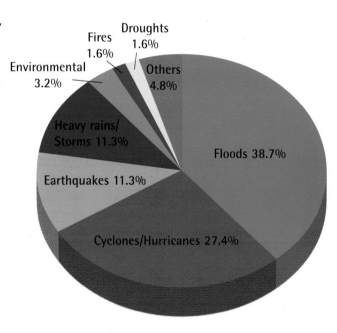

▲ This chart shows the percentage of different natural disasters that happened worldwide in 1996. The biggest percentage were floods.

A deadly hazard

Floods happen more often than any other natural disaster, such as earthquakes or hurricanes. A study of the 5,400 disasters that occurred worldwide from 1986–1995, showed that 30 per cent were caused by flooding. The study also reported that flooding had caused over half of the total number of lives lost.

Greatest damage
The continent of Asia suffers the greatest damage from flooding. From 1986 to 1995, it suffered 44 per cent of the world's flood disasters and 93 per cent of deaths from flooding. The death toll is high because so many people live on the flood-plains. In 1991, 140,000 people were killed by floods. The region also cannot afford to build effective flood defences.

Most often flooded
China is the country most often affected by flooding. It has suffered repeated flood disasters throughout the centuries. Chinese history describes how, in 2297 BC, massive rains burst the banks of the Yellow, Wei, and Yangtze Rivers, flooding almost the entire Northern China plain and turning the area into a huge inland sea.

FLOODS BRING DESTRUCTION

Entire villages are being swept away by floods in China as the situation along the swollen Yangtze river reaches a critical stage, Beijing has revealed. Hundreds of thousands of peasants are huddling for safety on the top of crumbling river banks.

Extract from *The Guardian*, 5 August 1998

The devastation

Flood waters can carry mud, earth and even large objects such as cars for long distances. The fast-moving waters can knock down bridges, shift houses and rip up anything not firmly held down. The kind of damage a flood causes depends on when it happens, how it happens, how far it reaches and how long it lasts.

Annual floods

In some areas, people have become used to small, frequently occurring floods. For example, the Ancient Egyptian settlers in the Nile valley welcomed the yearly flooding of the Nile River and used the waters to feed their crops.

However, unexpected floods can be severe and cause great damage, including the loss of many lives and the destruction of people's homes. Floods can also disrupt essential services, such as transport and electricity, pollute fresh water supplies and destroy crops.

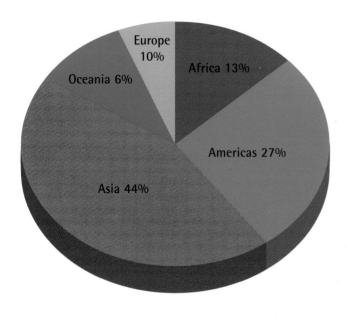

▲ This chart shows the percentage of floods worldwide by continent, 1987-1996.

This books investigates why floods happen. It looks at the damage they cause and what can be done to prevent it. It also looks at how the impact of climate change, global warming and human development may affect floods in the future.

◀ Damaged buildings and streets in Honduras, Central America, are evidence of the strength and power of flood waters.

The Movement of Water

Water is essential to all living things and without it the earth would be a lifeless planet. More than 90 per cent is held in the seas and oceans. The rest is on land in rivers, lakes, glaciers and ice-sheets.

Water moves all the time between air, land and sea. This continuous movement is known as the water cycle. It changes over time and from one place to another. The water cycle is an important part of hydrology (the science of water and flooding). Understanding how the water cycle works and the factors that control it is an important part of understanding the causes of floods.

The water cycle

The water cycle begins when water falls on to the earth's surface as rain or snow. This movement of water from the air to the land is called precipitation. More than half of this water quickly returns to the atmosphere through evaporation (the water turns into a gas) and transpiration (plants 'breathe' out the water).

▼ This diagram of the water cycle shows how water moves from one place to another.

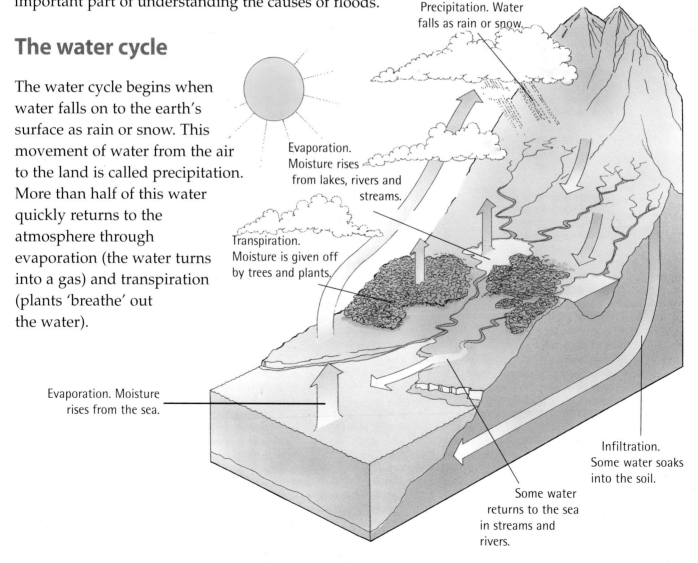

Precipitation. Water falls as rain or snow.

Evaporation. Moisture rises from lakes, rivers and streams.

Transpiration. Moisture is given off by trees and plants.

Evaporation. Moisture rises from the sea.

Infiltration. Some water soaks into the soil.

Some water returns to the sea in streams and rivers.

▲ Heavy rainfall in Ethiopia following a long period of drought causes soil and roads to be washed away.

Infiltration

Some of the water which remains on the earth's surface soaks into the soil. This is called infiltration and the speed at which this happens is called the infiltration rate. It sinks down until it reaches a layer full of water known as the water-table and travels through the ground as groundwater flow. Any water that is not soaked into the soil runs across the surface of the land and into streams and rivers. This is called surface runoff and is the main source of flood water.

The drainage basin

Floods are caused by the way an area of land is drained by its rivers and network of tributaries (small streams flowing into a large one). This area is called the drainage basin, or catchment. All drainage basins are different from one another.

The features

The different features of a drainage basin affect whether flooding might occur. These features include the size and shape of the basin, how it slopes, the type of soil and rocks it is made from, the amount of water held in the streams, and the speed at which the water flows. Other features are the type of vegetation in the drainage basin, and how the land is used by people. The area's climate (especially rainfall, temperature and speed of evaporation) is also important. All these features affect how the water is carried and how it drains away. For example, steeply sloping ground, thin soil and a cold climate all cause slow infiltration and so more surface runoff.

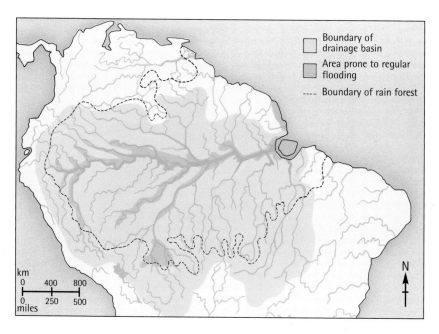

Boundary of drainage basin

Area prone to regular flooding

---- Boundary of rain forest

km
0   400   800

0   250   500
miles

N

▲ The river system and drainage basin of the fast-flowing Amazon River in South America.

A street in the town of La Grange, ▶ Missouri, USA, flooded when the river burst its banks in 1993.

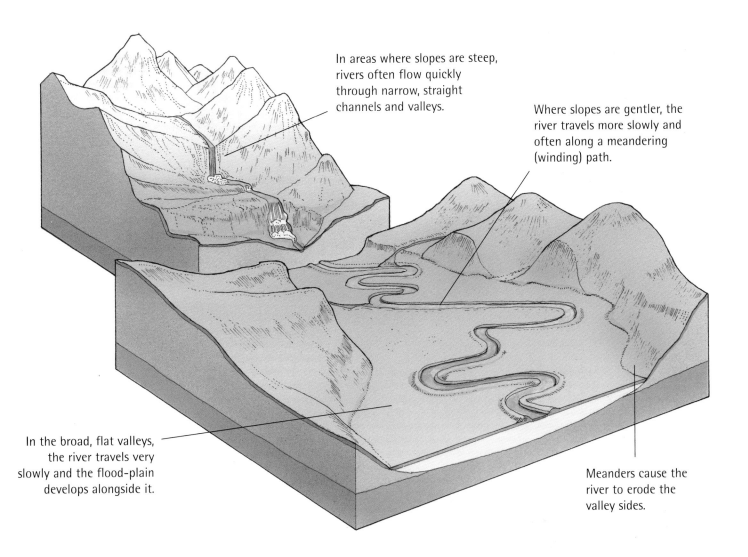

In areas where slopes are steep, rivers often flow quickly through narrow, straight channels and valleys.

Where slopes are gentler, the river travels more slowly and often along a meandering (winding) path.

In the broad, flat valleys, the river travels very slowly and the flood-plain develops alongside it.

Meanders cause the river to erode the valley sides.

▲ This diagram shows how a river changes as it flows from high ground to low ground.

River flow

The flow of the water in a river is called its discharge. Wide or deep rivers with fast-moving waters, such as the Amazon in South America, have a very high discharge.

Capacity

A river channel has a maximum amount of water that it can hold or carry along. This is called its capacity. The capacity of a channel depends on its shape and the river's discharge. If the channel's capacity is overloaded, then water will overflow the river banks and flooding will occur.

 DID YOU KNOW?

Flooding occurs when the water cycle is altered and produces too much water which is unable to escape in the usual ways.

What Causes River Floods?

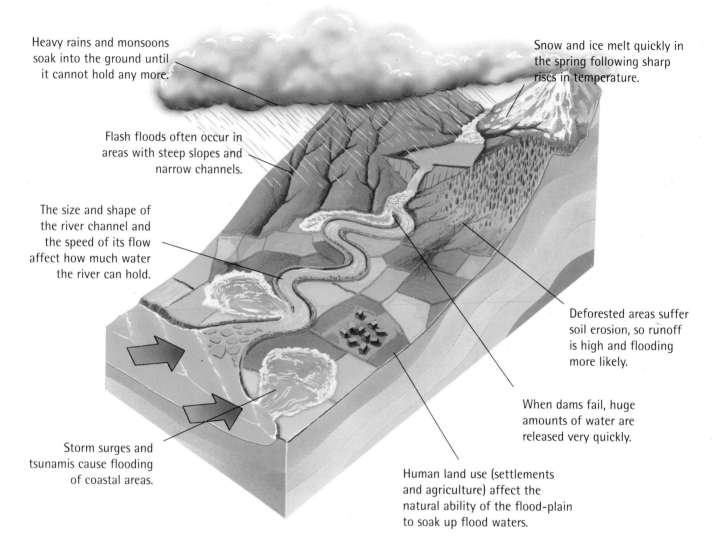

Heavy rains and monsoons soak into the ground until it cannot hold any more.

Snow and ice melt quickly in the spring following sharp rises in temperature.

Flash floods often occur in areas with steep slopes and narrow channels.

The size and shape of the river channel and the speed of its flow affect how much water the river can hold.

Deforested areas suffer soil erosion, so runoff is high and flooding more likely.

When dams fail, huge amounts of water are released very quickly.

Storm surges and tsunamis cause flooding of coastal areas.

Human land use (settlements and agriculture) affect the natural ability of the flood-plain to soak up flood waters.

A river flood occurs within the river's drainage basin and in river systems where tributaries may drain very large areas. During river floods, the river receives more water, mainly as surface runoff, than it can hold, with the result that it overflows.

▲ This diagram shows the different types of floods and how they are caused.

Heavy rainfall

High levels of rainfall are the most common cause of flooding. Rainfall floods often build up slowly and may last for days or weeks. In large, semi-arid countries, such as Australia, the rivers can carry flood waters hundreds of kilometres causing far distant dry riverbeds to flood weeks after heavy rainfall.

 DID YOU KNOW?

When floods are the result of prolonged rainfall, the flooding can last for over a week.

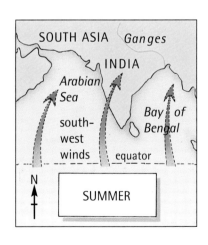

▲ Children fishing in the flooded streets of Thailand, south-east Asia. The floods were caused by heavy monsoon rains.

Long periods of heavy rain can cause dramatic, long-lasting floods. This is because the soil becomes too saturated (full) after a time to soak up any more water. The water then travels as surface runoff into streams and rivers which eventually overflow their banks.

During a cold winter, flooding may occur after lighter rainfall because frozen soil slows infiltration. There are also fewer plants to soak up rainwater through their roots.

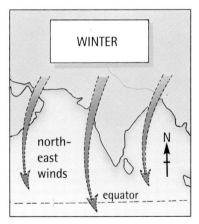

▲ In the summer rainy season, winds carry moisture from the sea inland, causing the torrential 'monsoon' rains. In the winter dry season, the winds blow in the opposite direction.

Monsoons

The word monsoon means 'season'. It originally applied to the wind system of the Arabian Sea, which blows for six months from the north-east direction and six months from the south-west. The south-west winds bring torrential rains to southern Asia and 'monsoon' now refers to this heavy rainfall. This often causes seasonal river flooding which drops sediment from the river bed onto the flood-plain, making the land so fertile that nearly half the world's population rely on the monsoon floods for their survival.

Flash floods

The name flash flood is given to a flood which occurs within six hours of the beginning of rainfall. Flash floods are violent, short-lived floods which are caused by surface runoff from torrential downpours. They can also happen when very large amounts of rain fall in a very short time, such as during a thunderstorm.

Flash floods can be very destructive because they always occur with only a few hours' warning. They are also fast-flowing and powerful, able to carry huge boulders and other large objects. In July 1997 in eastern Europe, flash floods following heavy rainfall swamped an area of over 60 square km, killing 49 people.

Hundreds of flash floods occur every year in the USA. They may last no longer than 15 minutes and rarely last more than 24 hours. They are especially threatening in steeply sloping areas, or in very dry places where the surface runoff is high and the river channels are shallow or narrow.

▼ This flash flood in Austria in 1988 had the power to rip up tree trunks and overturn cars.

▲ A flash-flood in the desert in Queensland, Australia.

▼ The flood that affected the Big Thompson Canyon.

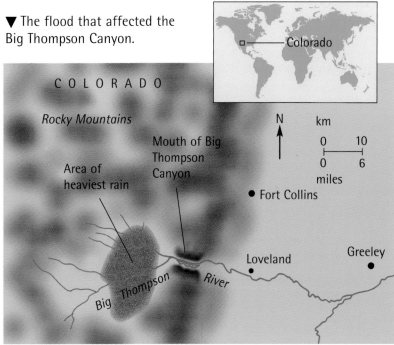

Big Thompson River, USA

A major flash flood occurred in July 1976 in the Big Thompson river valley in the Rocky Mountains, Colorado, USA. Over 30 cm of rain fell in four-and-a-half hours. The waters tore apart the local highway and threw up huge chunks of tarmac into the air. Houses, bridges and people were all swept away with the waters which were described as a 'raging torrent'. More than $35 million of damage was caused and 139 people were killed.

Lynmouth, Britain

In 1952, a dramatic flood caused by heavy rainfall occurred in the town of Lynmouth, Devon, Britain. Heavy rain had fallen for several weeks on to thin soil which had become saturated very quickly. On 15 August, 23 cm of rain fell in 24 hours. The rain ran into the rivers, which surged down the valley floors. The waters also transported trees and boulders which became trapped, creating temporary dams which later broke and caused more flooding. Most of Lynmouth's main street was destroyed by the waters – 91 houses and 100 vehicles were carried out to sea and 34 people were killed.

> 66 **EYEWITNESS** 99
>
> *"The whole mountainside is gone. There is no way. I'm trying to get out of here before I drown."*
>
> Patrolman William Miller's radio message, Big Thompson flood, 1976

A flooded farm in the town of Tiel in the Netherlands in 1995. The floods were caused by heavy rains and melting snow which caused the Waal River to burst its banks.

Snowmelt

A snowmelt flood is caused when snow thaws and water is suddenly released. The size of the flood depends on the amount of snow and the speed at which it melts. A depth of 100 cm of snow is roughly equivalent to 10 cm of rainfall. These floods usually occur annually in colder northern countries and mountainous regions when winter snows melt.

In 1948, the Fraser River in British Columbia, Canada, flooded. Heavy winter snows had been followed by a late, warm spring and the sudden high temperatures had caused rapid snowmelt. Prolonged flooding followed, lasting for more than a month.

In February 1999, a number of avalanches occurred in the Alps. They were caused by temperature changes and unusually heavy snowfall. The melting of the snow also caused severe flooding along the Rhine River and its tributaries in Germany and Switzerland.

Ice-jam

An ice-jam occurs when rivers freeze over and then thaw. The ice melts faster in some parts of the river than in others. This results in areas of high water levels trapped behind solid ice. When the ice finally melts, the water is released and flooding often results.

Dam failures

Dam floods happen when a dam collapses. Such floods are rare but when they do occur, huge amounts of water are released in very short periods of time, resulting in very violent floods and a lot of damage.

In about 3000 BC the world's first dam, the Sadd-el-Kafara in Egypt, failed during its first flood season. The failure is believed to have been due to design and construction faults. Many twentieth-century dam failures have been connected with construction faults.

In 1928, the 60-m-high St Francis dam in California, USA, collapsed drowning 400 people and causing more than $4 million of damage.

In October 1963, a landslide in Italy sent a huge quantity of rock into the reservoir above the Vaiont dam. This produced a wave of water which surged over the top of the dam, destroying everything in its path and killing 3,000 people. Amazingly, the dam was not seriously damaged.

▲ Workers attempt to clean up the wreckage in the streets following severe flooding in Germany.

DID YOU KNOW?

A flash flood In Johnstown, Pennsylvania, USA, in 1889 caused a dam to break, creating a 23-m-high wall of water which killed over 2,000 people in less than an hour.

What Causes Coastal Floods?

▼ This map shows some of the worst worldwide coastal floods and their causes.

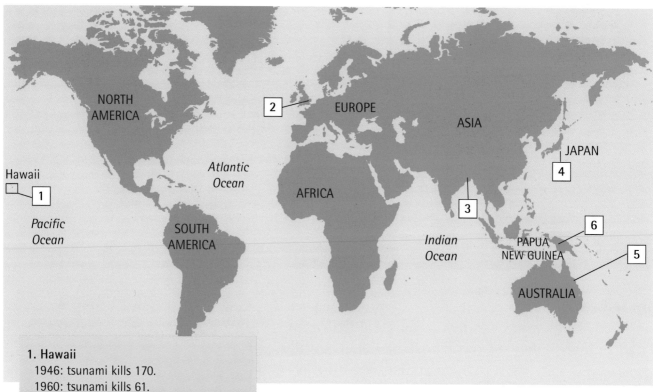

1. Hawaii
 1946: tsunami kills 170.
 1960: tsunami kills 61.

2. Netherlands and south-east England
 1953: storm surge causes flooding killing over 2,000.

3. Bangladesh
 1970: Cyclone causes coastal floods killing 3,000.

4. Japan
 1896: tsunami kills 26,000.

5. Australia
 1974: cyclone causes coastal flooding, affecting 45,000.

6. Papua New Guinea
 1998: tsunami kills 3,000.

Coastal areas flood when the land is invaded by the sea (see diagram on p. 12). This often happens when there are unusually high tides. If the flood areas are low-lying, the effects can be especially damaging. Most coastal floods happen when unusual weather conditions cause a storm surge which drives the sea inland. Flooding also happens when a tsunami caused by an earthquake or a volcanic eruption hits the coast.

Most low-lying coastal areas are already protected from normal high tides by sea-walls or embankments. However, these precautions are not enough if conditions are extreme. Low-lying areas will also suffer if the sea-level rises or the land subsides. When this happens, the land is slowly invaded (flooded) by the sea. This causes large areas of land to disappear and plant and animal habitats to be destroyed.

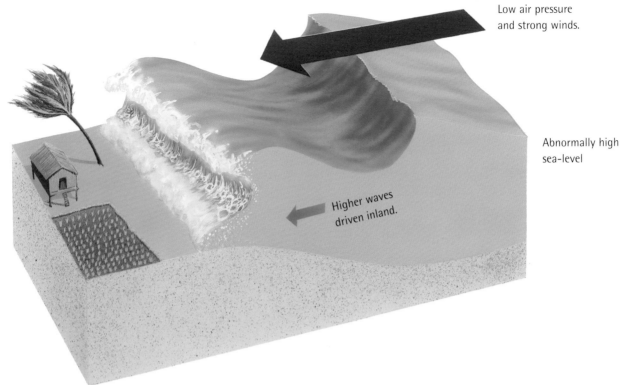

Low air pressure and strong winds.

Abnormally high sea-level

Higher waves driven inland.

▲ This diagram shows how a storm surge forces the sea on to the land.

Storm surges

A storm surge happens when low air pressure combines with strong winds. The low air pressure allows the sea-level to rise higher than normal and the winds force it on land. Storm surges can cause sea-levels to rise by up to 5 m. The storm which creates the surge may also bring with it heavy inland rainfall which makes the flooding even worse.

In some areas, hurricanes cause storm surges. Hurricanes are powerful, spinning winds which can be as much as 500 km in diameter and travel at up to 300 kph, faster than a high-speed train.

North Sea floods

In 1953, severe coastal flooding occurred in the Netherlands and south-east England. An intense storm created a surge which raised the sea-level by over 3 m, causing the collapse of coastal flood defences. More than 800 square km of land was flooded in Britain and there was widespread devastation in the Netherlands. Altogether, more than 2,200 people died and over 35,000 were evacuated. The cost of the damage was estimated to be more than £50 million.

> 66 **EYEWITNESS** 99
>
> *"We had to wade across, carrying our children and our possessions, from Canvey Island to the mainland. We thought the dog would drown after he ran off half way across, but luckily he turned up, looking rather dishevelled, two weeks later."*
>
> Floods survivor, south-east England, 1953

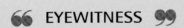

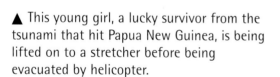

66 EYEWITNESS 99

"The wave hit in no time at all. It was dark. They were tumbled over and over with all the debris and iron and whatever. There was terrible confusion. They were washed one way and then the water turned around and went back again just as fast. (The survivors) are completely traumatized. They're hungry and thirsty. Three villages have been absolutely destroyed, with not a house standing. Two others have been badly devastated."

Father Austen Crapp, Australian missionary, Papua New Guinea

▲ This young girl, a lucky survivor from the tsunami that hit Papua New Guinea, is being lifted on to a stretcher before being evacuated by helicopter.

Tsunamis

A tsunami is a giant wave produced by an undersea earthquake, a volcanic eruption or a landslide. When one of these natural disasters occurs, huge amounts of energy are released, making the sea-bed shift and jolt and creating enormous shock waves which reach from the sea floor to the surface. Tsunamis are so powerful they can race across the ocean for thousands of kilometres at speeds of up to 800 kph.

The height of a tsunami depends on the depth of the water it is travelling through. In deep waters, tsunami surface waves are low and wide. But as they reach shallower waters close to the shore, the energy creates giant waves. Tsunamis can reach heights of 30 m or more (taller than 15 basketball players standing on one another's shoulders).

DID YOU KNOW?

The volcanic eruption of the island of Krakatoa in 1883 caused waves over 35 m high. These waves smashed into Java and Sumatra, killing over 36,000 people.

Papua New Guinea ⎯⎯ ▫

Papua New Guinea

On 17 July 1998, the north coast of Papua New Guinea in the Pacific Ocean was hit by three tsunami waves. The waves hit a 35-km stretch of the coast and the most powerful wave reached a height of more than 10 m. An earthquake measuring 7 on the Richter scale had caused the waves. It struck about 30 km away from the coast, which was hit by the waves less than four minutes later.

The huge waves swept more than 2 km inland, tearing up and flattening houses and trees and sucking debris into the ocean. At least seven villages were completely destroyed, 3,000 people were killed and many thousands missing or injured. In addition, bridges and airstrips were destroyed, which caused huge problems for the rescue operation.

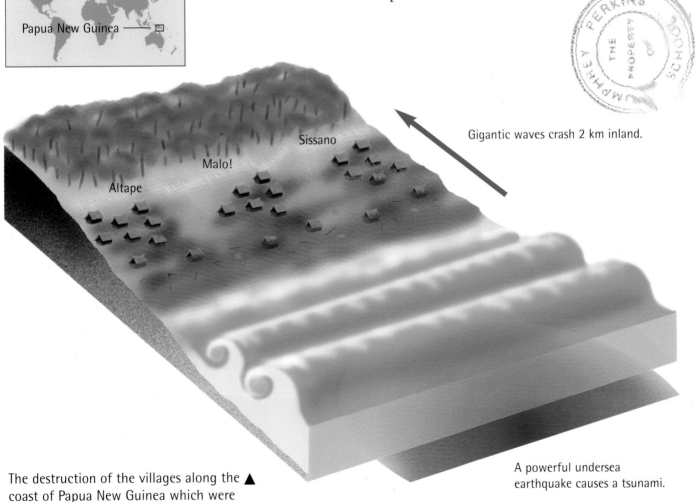

Gigantic waves crash 2 km inland.

Sissano

Malo!

Altape

The destruction of the villages along the ▲ coast of Papua New Guinea which were swamped by three huge tsunami waves, the last of which was more than 10 m high.

A powerful undersea earthquake causes a tsunami.

The Human Factor

The major developments on the flood-plains designed to meet human needs include land-drainage, building roads, bridges and housing, and farming practices such as deforestation and overgrazing. These changes increase the chances of flooding by slowing down the infiltration of water and causing coastal areas to subside.

Urbanization

Many of the world's greatest cities are built on the banks of rivers or at river deltas. These locations were chosen for their water supply and fertile land which is also flat and so easier to develop.

Subsidence

Most of the world's flat coastal areas are subsiding naturally, but the balance is kept even by the natural dumping of sediments whenever a flood happens. However, when a coastal area is developed or a river is dammed, the land no longer receives new sediment to balance the subsidence. In addition, the weight of human development can make matters worse. Subsiding areas will gradually flood or be invaded by coastal waters.

SILTING CAUSES FLOOD

Details of a disaster in Li county are coming to light. More than 30 people died, 60 are missing, 46,000 houses were destroyed and 80,000 people are living in shanties on top of the dikes. The Li river, which burst its banks, flows into the Dongting lake near Yueyang, which in normal times absorbs excess water from the Yangtze river. But the lake has silted up in recent years as the population upstream has increased and marshland has been drained.

Extract from *The Guardian*, 5 August 1998

◄ The silted-up Dongting Lake, part of the Yangtze River system, has been drained and reclaimed for agricultural use.

▲ Flooding in the streets of Kuala Lumpur, Malaysia demonstrates the huge impact of urbanization and the building of roads and paved areas.

 DID YOU KNOW?
Each year, flooding in India causes losses of more than 700 lives and costs of £60 million in repairs.

Increased runoff

Buildings, roads and paved areas make infiltration more difficult, causing rapid runoff. The networks of drains and gutters in cities are designed to carry this runoff to the rivers as quickly as possible. The result is that cities send more water at greater speed into the rivers than is natural. Bridges, docks, buildings and artificial river management schemes, such as canals, may also alter the flow of the water.

Deforestation

Forests soak up huge quantities of rainfall and allow it to filter slowly into the ground. If trees are cut down, the rain falls directly on to the ground where it cannot be infiltrated quickly enough. Instead, it runs straight off the slopes, carrying with it the loose soil no longer held together by tree roots. The surface runoff and soil flow into the rivers and streams, clogging them with sediment. The rivers and streams cannot hold as much water and are more likely to overflow.

Flood Disasters

A HARD RAIN

It was on Tuesday evening that the good people of St. Louis came closest to despair. Even though rain was still sluicing down and more was forecast, they had been assured on Sunday that the Mississippi, the mighty river surging out of control through their city, had 'crested' when it reached a record height of 46.9 ft (14.2 m). On Monday, as predicted, the level fell. Then at 5pm on Tuesday, a mile-long stretch of the 15ft (4.5m) levee holding back the swollen waters of the river Des Peres collapsed and part of a suburb of pleasant bungalows in the south of St Louis was flooded. In normal times, the river is no more than a narrow stream a couple of feet wide which feeds into the Mississippi.

Extract from *The Sunday Times*, 25 July 1993

Flood disasters can happen wherever people are prepared to put themselves and their livelihoods at risk.

Mississippi, USA

In July 1993, the Mississippi flood-plain was affected by one of the worst natural disasters ever to hit the USA. It was the worst flooding for seventy years and greater than any other flood in terms of the amount of rainfall, the high river levels and the vast area flooded. The flood lasted for over a month. A huge number of people were affected, crops were destroyed and property damaged.

The flood

The flooding was the result of unusual weather conditions. A wet autumn was followed by heavy snowfall in the winter and heavy spring rains. The combination of rapid melting of winter snow and heavy rainfall led to local flooding in March. However, the wet weather continued and flooding became widespread in June. During July, the two biggest rivers in the region, the Missouri and the Mississippi, broke through their flood defences. The waters did not begin to disappear until mid-August.

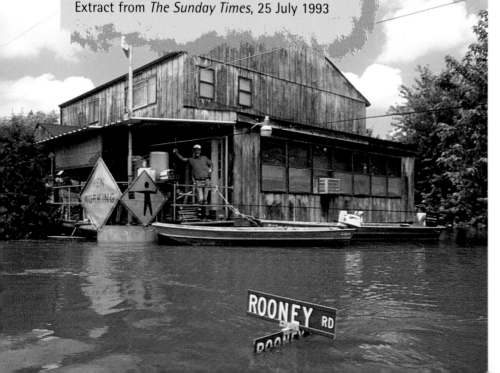

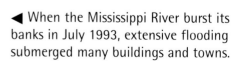

◄ When the Mississippi River burst its banks in July 1993, extensive flooding submerged many buildings and towns.

The damage

The impact of the flood waters was huge. An area of over 80,000 square km was flooded, transport and communications could not function, and the Mississippi was closed to shipping for two months. Luckily, due to good warning systems, the death toll was fewer than fifty people. However, 54,000 people were evacuated, about 75 towns were completely devastated and 35,000 homes were destroyed. The financial losses and cost of clearing up and rebuilding was valued at approximately $15–20 billion.

▼ Levee walls, one of the protection measures built in an attempt to make the Mississippi region safe from flooding.

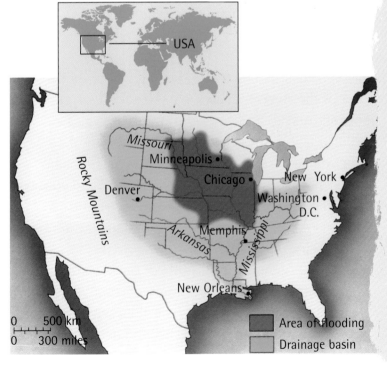

USA

Missouri
Minneapolis
Denver
Chicago
New York
Washington D.C.
Arkansas
Memphis
Rocky Mountains
Mississippi
New Orleans

0   500 km
0   300 miles

■ Area of flooding
■ Drainage basin

Lessons learned

For over fifty years, engineers had tried to make the Mississippi region safe from flooding. Protection measures included building solid defences such as dams, reservoirs and barrages. However, it was obvious after the flood of 1993 that these defences were not enough to deal with such a severe flood. People wondered whether these protective measures had actually made the situation worse. In areas where solid flood barriers have been built, the structures can disrupt the flood's natural path across the flood-plain and so interfere with its ability to soak up the waters. It was also thought that some parts of the plains were actually sinking from the weight of the structures. The authorities realized they must consider protection schemes which do not rely on solid structures. Towns and buildings were also rebuilt away from the flood-prone areas.

◀ Villagers wade through the floodwaters in Kerani ganj, Bangladesh, following the flooding in 1998.

Bangladesh, Asia

Bangladesh lies in the delta region of three major rivers: the Ganges, the Brahmaputra and the Meghna. Much of Bangladesh is very low-lying and over 80 per cent of the land consists of flood-plains, which are home to most of the country's 120 million people. About a quarter of the country is flooded each year during the summer monsoons (see p. 13).

The flood

During 1998, the flooding was more widespread and damaging than usual. This was because the heavy summer monsoon rains happened at the same time as severe weather in the Bay of Bengal. The resulting storm surges created high tides which prevented the flood waters from draining away into the sea. This meant the floods lasted for much longer than usual.

The damage

The 1998 Bangladesh floods were considered the worst of the twentieth century. Although severe flooding in 1988 had caused more deaths and a similar portion of the country was flooded, the waters disappeared after only three weeks. In 1998, the floods covered over three-quarters of the country and lasted for more than two months. More than 1,100 people were killed and more than 30 million were affected. Damage was done to 15,000 km of roads, 14,000 schools, hundreds of bridges and 500,000 homes. It was impossible to calculate the scale of the damage and the cost of clearing up. In addition, as the flood waters drained away, the problems of mud, famine and disease took over.

> ## 66 EYEWITNESS 99
>
> *"In October last year there was no monsoon, so the rice harvest failed. That was followed by a severe winter, leading to the failure of vegetable crops. The rice harvest this spring was only average. Now the summer flood means there will be no harvest at all in November. From now onwards, gruel kitchens will the the only way to prevent famine, because people in the flooded areas no longer have money to buy food."*
>
> Nayeem Wahra, aid worker, Bangladesh, 1998

INDIA

BANGLADESH

Dhaka

Chandpur

Madaripur

Khulna

Barisal

Calcutta

Bay of Bengal

km
0   50
0   30
miles

Indian
Ocean

Bangladesh

Key

○ Villages destroyed
by floods

■ Area worst-affected
by floods

▼ Children collecting drinking water supplied by emergency aid as flooding had polluted supplies.

Lessons learned

The effects of the flooding were worsened by the huge population. Although the fertile land is able to feed everyone, the ever-increasing population has led to more development which has created more roads and buildings to be destroyed. To prevent even more damage from floods in the future, this development needs to be controlled. Also, the area contains a number of different flood-plains, which are affected by the flood waters in different ways. Flood prevention measures suitable for these different areas need to be put in place, as one standard measure cannot provide overall protection.

Hurricane Mitch, Central America

On 28 October 1998, Hurricane Mitch struck Central America. It was considered to be the most destructive hurricane for 200 years. Wind-speeds of over 300 kph were recorded and 60 cm of rain (over 15 times more than usual) fell for several days. The flooding and mudslides that followed caused widespread destruction.

The damage

The worst-hit regions were the countries of Honduras and Nicaragua. Honduras was almost entirely covered in water. Over 100 bridges, 80 per cent of the roads and 75 per cent of the farmland was destroyed. The banana plantations were devastated, destroying the country's main source of wealth. Over 5,000 people are believed to have died, 12,000 were missing and 250,000 made homeless. The cost of the damage to Honduras was estimated at up to $2 billion.

66 EYEWITNESS 99

"We were asleep when the fire brigade came with loudspeakers to tell us the river was rising and we should get out. At first, we took no notice, but then the earth started to move. I grabbed my children and ran. All we have now are the clothes we've been given."

Bianca Rosa Andrade, flood victim, Honduras 1998

▼ Residents of La Lima in Honduras rescue their belongings during the evacuation of the town, following the flooding from the torrential rains caused by Hurricane Mitch.

At least half of Nicaragua was also affected, with over 1,300 casualties, more than 3,000 people missing and 750,000 made homeless. The collapse of the water-filled volcanic crater of Casita made conditions worse. The lava and water formed a huge mudslide which buried a village.

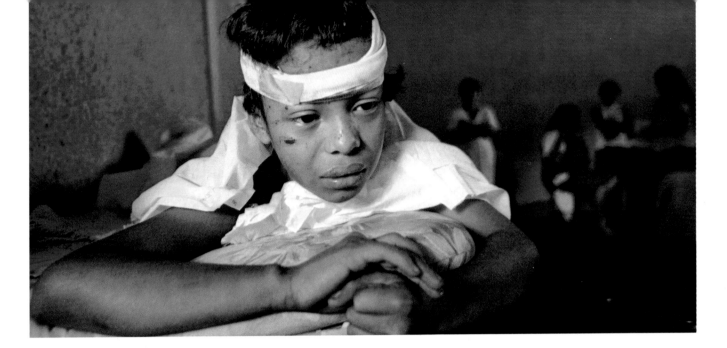

▲ One of the lucky children rescued from the mudslide caused by the collapse of the Casitas volcano is cared for in an emergency shelter.

Central America

N

Key

Worst flooding

MEXICO

km

0   500

0   300
            miles

Caribbean Sea

GUATEMALA

HONDURAS

EL SALVADOR

NICARAGUA

• Managua

path of hurricane

COSTA RICA

Casita volcano cone collapsed, causing a mudslide which killed over 1,000 people.

Pacific Ocean

Throughout Central America damage was widespread. The rising rivers tore through bridges and roads and destroyed crops, houses, hospitals and schools. Efforts to rescue survivors and provide food, shelter and clean water were badly slowed by the damage. Several large cities in Honduras became islands, reached only by air.

At least 11,000 people were reported killed and thousands went missing. The true number may never be known because many bodies were buried under metres of mud. More than 3 million people lost their homes and their livelihoods. The costs of the damage are estimated to be as high as $5 billion. It is thought that the clear-up operation could take decades.

Lessons learned

The region had been completely unprepared. Although the hurricane was predicted, the forecast had shown that it would turn west instead of south and rainfall and flooding had not been considered. When the official warning finally came, it failed due to the region's poor communications. In the future, hurricane forecasts need to be more accurate and should consider the effects of rainfall and severe weather. Effective flood warning and communications systems are also essential.

▲ A family standing amongst the remains of their house, which was washed away in the floods that hit China in the summer of 1998.

China

During the summer of 1998, torrential rainfall in China caused massive flooding. The heaviest rainfall was in Qinzhou, where 173 cm fell during June and July. The Yangtze river and its tributaries rose to its highest levels since 1954, when floods killed more than 30,000 people.

Official reports said this was one of the worst floods to hit China for 130 years. Entire villages were swept away, and an area of over 500,000 square km was destroyed or damaged. The death toll was over 3,700 people and a further 14 million were left homeless. A total of 240 million people were affected by the floods in some way. Over $80 billion of damage was caused.

GREAT WALL OF WATER

In front of us stand a mother with her baby, her five-year-old-son and his grandmother. Behind them is a scene of utter devastation. Where once there were houses there is a featureless expanse of silt and rubble. They explain what happened: how the rains were incessant. How they were warned to leave their house and move to the flood shelter. How the river level rose 11 m in one day. How the pregnant mother was trampled in a stampede when it looked like the shelter itself was going to be inundated. How some people refused to leave the houses that sheltered behind the 15m-high-dike. And then, they describe the catastrophic 10 seconds during which the dike gave way and the liquid explosion which followed not simply flattening the houses but destroying the buildings and the very ground on which they stood.

Report by Edward Parker for WWF, Central Yangtze region, China, March 1999

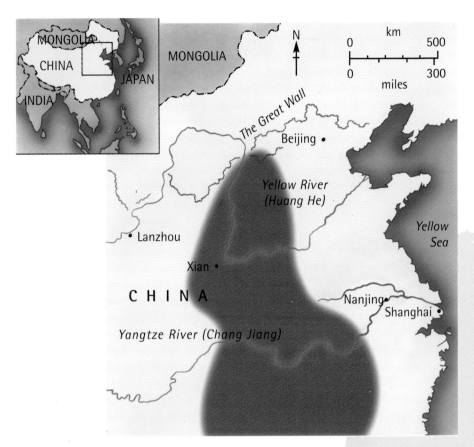

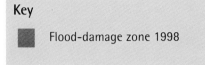

Key

Flood-damage zone 1998

Lessons learned

The flood season is expected in China. As in Bangladesh, China's large population inhabits the flood-plains. However, the flooding is becoming more widespread and seems to be out of control. The Chinese government had blamed unusual weather. However, after the 1998 floods they admitted that years of bad land management, especially deforestation, had played a big part in the flood disasters. Since 1949, thousands of trees in the upper regions of the Yangtze River had been cut down. By 1986, the tree cover had dropped from 86 per cent to under 10 per cent. To improve the situation, the government put a ban on deforestation and re-employed the loggers to plant new trees.

◄ This reed bed in Lake Dongting benefits the population by providing raw materials for local paper mills. It also adds to the build-up of silt in the lake, a major cause of flooding.

Benefits of Floods

Although floods can cause devastation and great damage, they bring benefits too. Many ancient civilizations flourished on the flood-plains, including the Mesopotamians in the Tigris and Euphrates river valleys, and the Egyptians in the Nile delta.

The Nile delta

The flood waters of the Nile delta in Egypt have guaranteed water to grow crops for more than 5,000 years. The Nile is the world's longest river and floods twice each year as a result of the monsoons.

For many years, the Egyptians have used different irrigation schemes so that the flood waters in the delta can be used to water the land. The irrigation schemes also stored water for use in a drought, and allowed crop production to keep up with population growth.

▼ The Aswan dam, built in the 1960s, controls the flow of the Nile river. Excess waters are stored in the Lake Nasser reservoir.

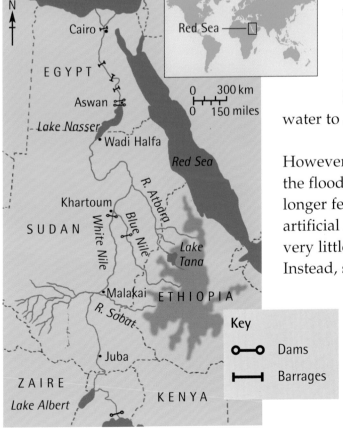

▲ Downstream of the Aswan dam, the Nile provides water to irrigate almost all of the farmland in the area.

The Aswan dam

When the Aswan dam was built in the 1960s, it was believed it would bring the flood waters under control and end the crop failures caused by the floods and droughts which occurred in the area. Its most important feature is the Lake Nasser reservoir, which can store more water than the annual flow of the Nile. The Nile's flow downstream of the dam is the country's major irrigation canal. Its flow is fully controlled and the local irrigation channels which branch off carry water to about 95 per cent of farmland.

However, the dam has also caused problems. By storing the flood waters, the sediments from the river bed no longer fertilize the plains and farmers have had to use artificial fertilizers. Controlling the flow also means that very little water is reaching the Nile delta and the sea. Instead, sea-water is 'creeping' into the delta sediments and poisoning the soil and groundwater with salt. Finally, the Nile delta is subsiding. This is partly due to the weight of development and partly to the loss of sediment deposits. As a result, Egypt is losing valuable land.

◄ The barrages and dams of the Nile river.

The Everglades

This vast wetland (marshland) area in Florida, USA, formed over 5,000 years ago as a result of summer-storm flooding. It creates a unique habitat for plants and animals and is the only system of its kind in the world. Although the region was nearly destroyed by human development, it is now considered to be of great importance and is a huge tourist attraction.

Before human development changed it, the river was spread over 4 million hectares. It created a patchwork of different habitats, including ponds, marshes, swamps and forests. Unusual plants and animals lived there, including alligators, snakes and the Florida panther. In the nineteenth century, draining and land development started. Large areas were transformed by canals, roads, fields and buildings. Today, only 50 per cent of the original wetland areas exist.

▲ The Everglades is a shallow freshwater river, less than 2 m deep and 80 km wide. It looks like a huge sheet of water and flows slowly south (about 30 m per day) from the Kissimmee River to Florida Bay.

 DID YOU KNOW?
The Everglades is one of only three sites in the world declared an International Biosphere Reserve, a World Heritage Site and a Wetland of International Importance.

An important ecosystem

Fortunately today the area is protected as a National Park. Development is no longer allowed and some land is being returned to its wetland state. The Everglades acts as a natural barrier between the sea and southern Florida's towns and cities. It has open wetlands, human-made and natural lakes, and waterways. It has also been separated into managed areas, so water movement during floods and droughts can be controlled.

▼ These alligators are one example of the rare creatures and plants which live in the Everglades National Park.

The restoration of the Everglades balances the needs of the natural ecosystem with the needs of the people of southern Florida. Water management is essential, since the water that supports the plants and animals of the Everglades also supports the people in the cities. In addition, flood protection for the developed areas must be balanced with the need to protect the wildlife habitats.

SOUTH FLORIDA

Gulf of Mexico

Big Cypress National Preserve

Miami

Everglades National Park

Atlantic Ocean

Florida

Predicting Floods

Although it is impossible to prevent floods, we know in which areas flooding is likely to happen. By putting protection and prediction schemes in place, flood damage can be dramatically reduced.

Flood warnings

Scientists produce a flood forecast using a computer model which predicts how a river system will react to various weather conditions. The latest data on such factors as rainfall, cloud cover and river height is fed into the model which then forecasts how the river will respond.

Information gathering

A lot of information on weather conditions including rainfall, cloud cover and humidity comes from radar and satellite systems. Other information, such as river height, air temperature and wind speed and direction, is collected at ground stations.

Radar detects and measures clouds and precipitation using high-frequency sound waves. The information is transmitted to a computer which uses different colours to show the rates of rainfall in different places.

MEASURING RIVER FLOW

Scientists create a hydrograph to give a picture of changes in river discharge (volume and speed) over a period of time. Storm and flood hydrographs compare rainfall with stream-flow.

Discharge (cubic metres per second)

Peak flow

River level drops

Storm flow

Peak rainfall

Normal river level

Rainfall

Rainfall   Day 1   Day 2   Day 3

TIME

▲ This infra-red satellite image shows the extent of the flooded lake, Dongting Hu, in China in 1998, which destroyed over 5 million houses. The water is in blue, the vegetation in red.

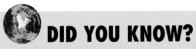 **DID YOU KNOW?**

By 1985, one in twenty communities in the USA had its own flood-warning system.

Weather satellites carry on-board instruments called radiometers that produce pictures which are transmitted back to scientists on earth. They create visible-light images of the earth and its cloud-cover. These instruments also transmit infra-red pictures, based on heat measurements, to show the temperature and height of the cloud cover.

All the information is collected and put into a computer model to produce a forecast. If the forecast shows that conditions may result in a flood, a flood warning will be issued.

Mapping

Flood-plain maps are designed to predict the size and extent of a future flood and when it might happen. They are produced from records of past floods and aerial photographs. These maps help scientists to set up the right protection measures for an area.

Protection schemes

Flood protection schemes are built to protect an area against floods that are certain to return. The length of time between one flood and the next is called the return period. Floods with large return periods happen less often, but are likely to cause worse flooding. Many areas in the USA have flood protection schemes designed to withstand floods with a hundred-year return period. More precautions are taken where there is a big risk to human life, so dams are often designed to stand up to floods with return periods of 10,000 years!

There are two main methods of flood protection: stopping or controlling flooding with structures such as dikes or dams; or controlling building and development on the flood-plain so there is less flood damage.

Structural control

Dikes, or levees, are earth banks built along the sides of rivers to stop an overflow of flood water. They allow the river to flow deeper and faster. They are not usually able to control large floods. If built near to the river banks, they are liable to erosion (wearing away) and may break down.

DAM WILL STOP FLOODS

"If we had the Three Gorges Dam, the levels in the lower reaches of the Yangtze would not be so high, and the situation would not be so urgent," said Zao Chunming of the State Flood Control and Drought Relief Headquarters, Beijing. Opponents of the dam disagree, saying that its on-going construction has lulled flood officials into a false sense of security, and that restoration work on dikes and embankments has suffered as a result. The dam will not be fully operational for another decade at least.

Extract from *The Independent*, 7 August 1998

◀ The Kariba dam and the man-made lake behind it. The dam was built to protect the area from flooding. The lake provides a store for the floodwaters and the dam allows the water to be released more slowly.

▲ The Thames Barrier was completed in the 1980s and was built to protect London from flooding. It has ten steel gates which can be raised to block the river when danger threatens.

Dams and flood-control reservoirs store flood waters and release them slowly. Although the flooding lasts for longer, it is at a lower, safer level. The reservoir can also supply hydro-electric power (electricity using energy from water) or water for irrigation.

The Thames Barrier

The Thames Barrier is a tidal defence system designed to protect London from flooding. It was constructed after flooding caused by a storm surge devastated south-east England in 1953. During the flood, the Thames rose by over a metre, breaking through protective embankments.

River training methods include altering river channels to carry water away more quickly and efficiently. Channels may be deepened, widened or straightened. Extra flood-diversion channels can also be built.

Building and development control

Some safety precautions are based on controlling the development on the flood-plain. They include land-use planning, floodproofing, soil and water conservation, and accurate forecasts and warnings. Land-use planning is the most important measure. It pinpoints zones where certain types of development might increase the risk of flooding. Floodproofing protects roads, homes, water-treatment plants, communications networks and power supplies. Buildings can be located outside the flood-prone area, raised above the flood-plain, or built with concrete or steel flood walls.

▼ The different measures that can be used to protect people and land from flooding.

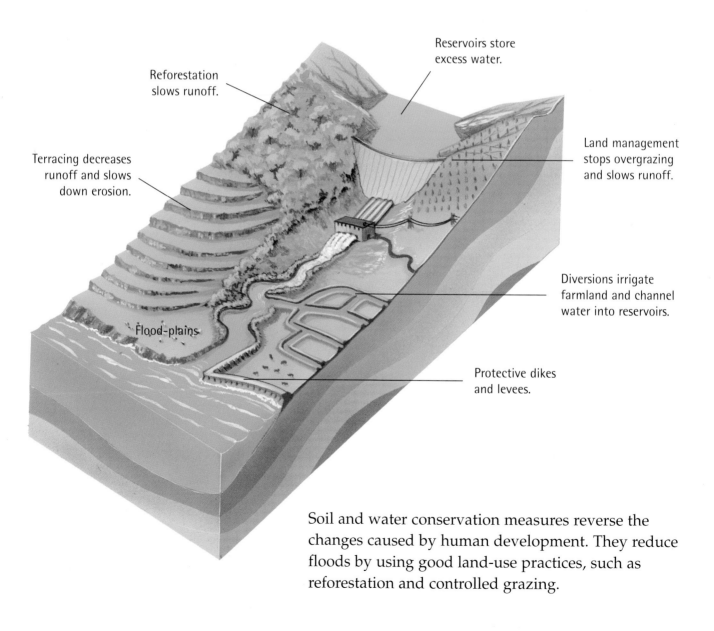

Reservoirs store excess water.

Reforestation slows runoff.

Terracing decreases runoff and slows down erosion.

Land management stops overgrazing and slows runoff.

Diversions irrigate farmland and channel water into reservoirs.

Flood-plains

Protective dikes and levees.

Soil and water conservation measures reverse the changes caused by human development. They reduce floods by using good land-use practices, such as reforestation and controlled grazing.

EYEWITNESS

"We are expecting cholera, epidemics of dengue fever, diarrhoea, bacterial fevers and malaria. People who are weak anyway will suffer greatly. There are hundreds of communities where we have not even made contact. Many are several days by horse. We may never know the toll or the damage done."

Local official, Honduras, Central America

▼ This bridge was washed away during the floods caused by Hurricane Mitch. The supply of help and relief to the area was badly affected by the damage to the transport and communication systems, which prevented rescue teams from reaching the devastated areas.

Structural or non-structural?

Early flood management schemes relied on structural barriers for protection. However, large structures are expensive to build and maintain. They also change the river's natural flow which can affect the environment. Today, environment-friendly, less expensive, non-structural methods are preferred

The after-effects

When a flood happens, a good emergency response system is needed to give immediate help. Rescue teams, evacuation centres and hospitals must be prepared. In addition, the after-effects of a flood can sometimes be worse than the flood itself. When the waters disappear, huge amounts of mud are left behind; peoples' homes and belongings are ruined; farmland is destroyed and essential supplies such as electricity or gas are damaged. If it takes a long time to clear up the damage and restore services, then the combination of mud, polluted water and lack of resources may cause disease and starvation.

Global Warming and El Niño

During the twentieth century, the number of flooding disasters has increased. Forecasts show that future floods will threaten over 500 million people worldwide. Bangkok, Hong Kong, Tokyo, Rio de Janeiro and Venice are all vulnerable cities. Recent studies are examining the possible impact of global warming and El Niño on flooding, since it is believed they have large effects on the environment.

Global warming and the greenhouse effect

The greenhouse effect is caused by the sun's rays and carbon dioxide and other gases in the atmosphere. Like the glass in a greenhouse, the greenhouse gases allow the sun's rays through to heat the earth but trap some of the heat as it radiates back. This natural greenhouse effect causes global warming which keeps the earth warmer than it would otherwise be and is essential for life on earth to survive.

However, the earth today is suffering from abnormal global warming. Many believe that human development is to blame and that industrial pollution and vehicle exhaust fumes have increased the levels of greenhouse gases in the atmosphere. As a result, the ground temperature has increased by 0.5 °C.

▲ The city of Rio de Janeiro, in Brazil, is just one of the major cities in the world likely to suffer from flooding in the future.

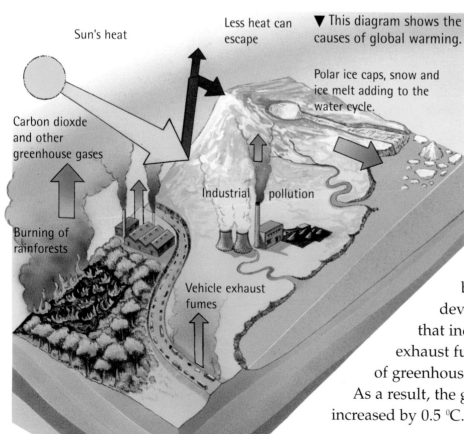

Sun's heat

Less heat can escape

▼ This diagram shows the causes of global warming.

Polar ice caps, snow and ice melt adding to the water cycle.

Carbon dioxde and other greenhouse gases

Industrial pollution

Burning of rainforests

Vehicle exhaust fumes

The international organization IPCC, Intergovernmental Panel on Climate Change) has forecast that average global temperatures could rise by about 3⁰C and that sea-levels could rise by as much as 66 cm by 2100. This could have huge impacts on coastal areas and weather systems.

Global warming and the weather

It has been predicted that rising temperatures from global warming could speed up the water cycle. Evaporation rates could increase and the weather could become more unpredictable. Forecasts suggest that in future, rainfall will increase in northern countries and also during the summer monsoon causing worse flooding. In addition dry areas, such as in southern Europe, could have less rainfall and suffer more drought and heat waves.

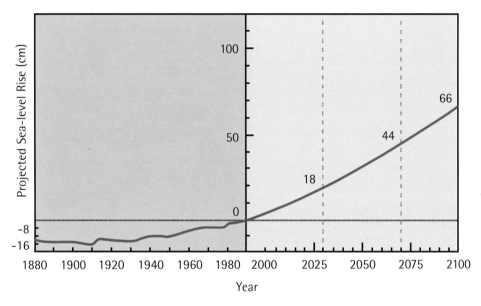

Historical: Record of sea-level rise   Forecast: Rise under current conditions

▲ This graph predicts the rate at which the sea-level will rise by the end of the twenty-first century.

Sea-level rise

The predicted sea-level rise will happen because of an increase in the volume of the oceans. This is because warm water takes up more space than cold water. It is also thought that small land glaciers in the Arctic and the Greenland ice-sheet will melt. However; the impact of global warming on the Antarctic ice-sheet is unclear. Some scientists argue that the ice-sheet will break up and melt, causing higher sea-levels. Others suggest that heavier rainfall will cause more ice to form which could mean that the ice-sheet will grow and cause sea-levels to drop.

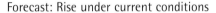

▲ Severe droughts in Brazil during 1997 and 1998 believed to be caused by El Niño, have caused many crops to fail. These children are walking through the dry countryside in search of water.

El Niño

El Niño is the name given to the switch in direction and strength of ocean currents and winds in the Pacific Ocean. It usually occurs every three to seven years and may last from several months to more than a year.

The effects of El Niño have been linked to changes in temperatures, storm patterns and rainfall worldwide. El Niño was even blamed for the poor prediction of Hurricane Mitch.

The 1997–1998 El Niño event was long-lasting and caused severe climate changes across the world. They included droughts in East Africa, Australia and Brazil and heavy rains in California, South America and Sri Lanka. Scientists fear that global warming will increase El Niño conditions.

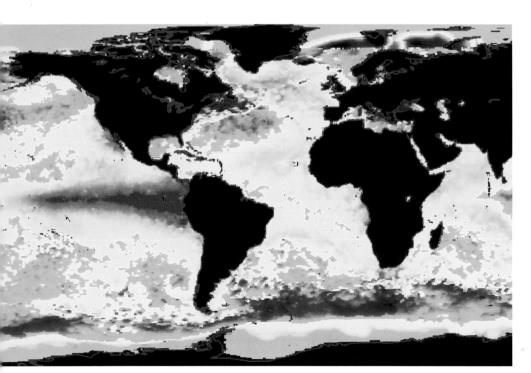

▲ A satellite image of the El Niño event of 1997 clearly shows the area of abnormally warm surface water (in red) off the coast of South America.

The future

There is no clear picture of how global warming and El Niño will influence our future climate or what impact they will have on floods. However, an increased threat from flood damage depends also on human impact.

Building towns and cities, deforestation and farming make flooding worse and as human development grows in coastal areas, subsidence levels also increase. Nearly half the world's population lives within 60 km of the coastline. In particular, Bangladesh, Egypt, Nigeria and Thailand are all losing land to the sea.

CITY AWAITS THE FLOOD

This time it was a routine flood. It was not The Flood, the catastrophic event that strikes St Petersburg once in a century. When The Flood comes it will wreak havoc on the lives and cultural treasures of the city...
"I looked at the water and thought, thank God it's changed direction," said Sergei Burdukov. "Because, despite all our preparations, we're not prepared."

Extract from *The Guardian*, March 1999

Environmental awareness

As human development has increased, so has our awareness of its effects on the environment. For example in China, where deforestation has made flooding worse, the government has put a ban on logging and has re-employed the loggers to plant trees.

As long as we continue to consider the effects of human impacts on the environment, successful flood protection and prevention measures will be put in place to minimize the damage from floods, whatever the weather.

▼ Parts of Baja, California, USA, received twice the normal rainfall during the 1997–98 El Niño event, filling streams and causing flooding.

Glossary

Capacity The amount of water a river can store.

Discharge A river's flow, calculated from the amount of water and the speed at which it is travelling.

Deforestation Cutting down trees.

Delta Low-lying flat land where a river divides into channels that flow into the sea.

Drainage basin The area of land drained by a river system.

Ecosystem A community of plants and animals and the environment they inhabit.

El Niño The name given to the change in sea currents and winds in the Pacific Ocean that occurs every three to seven years and affects world weather patterns.

Evaporation When water turns into a gas and rises into the air.

Flash flood A sudden flood which starts very soon after rainfall.

Flood-plain The low-lying flat land next to a river where it floods and drops sediment.

Flood return period The average time period between floods of a certain size.

Greenhouse effect The trapping of the sun's warmth around the earth by carbon dioxide and other greenhouse gases.

Groundwater Water that soaks into the soil and cracks in underground rock.

Hydrograph A graph that measures changes in a river's discharge over a period of time.

Hydrology The study of water.

Infiltration The flow of water through the soil.

Irrigation scheme A water supply carried by artificial channels or streams.

Monsoon The rainy season in south-east Asia when winds blow rains in from the sea.

Precipitation Rain or snow falling to the ground.

River system The network of streams and tributaries that make up the drainage basin.

Sediments River mud, rich in nutrients, that is deposited on the land during floods.

Snowmelt floods Floods caused when snow and ice melts rapidly, making river channels overflow.

Storm surge Unusually high seas caused by low air pressure which are then blown on to land by strong winds.

Subsidence Sinking of land.

Surface run-off Water that flows along the surface of the ground into a river.

Transpiration Water vapour that rises into the air from the leaves of plants and trees.

Tributary A small river that flows into a larger river.

Tsunami A giant ocean wave caused by an undersea earthquake or volcanic eruption.

Water cycle The movement of water between air, land and sea.

Wetlands An area of land saturated with water, also known as a swamp or marsh.

Further information

BOOKS

A closer look at Tidal Waves and Flooding (Watts)

Against the Elements: Water (Watts, 1999)

Focus on Disasters: Floods by Fred Martin (Heinemann, 1995)

Natural Disasters by David Alexander (UCL Press, London, 1995)

Repairing the damage: Fires & Floods by David Lambert (Evans, 1997)

Restless Earth: Floods and Tidal Waves by Terry Jennings (Belitha Press, 1999)

The Earth Strikes Back: Water by Pamela Grant and Arthur Haswell (Belitha Press, 1999)

Weird Weather by Paul Simons (Warner Books, London, 1997)

CD-ROMS

Interfact: Weather (Worldaware, 1999) PC and MAC versions available. Looks at the water cycle, wind, snow, droughts and seasons as well as floods.

Violent Earth, (Wayland Multimedia, 1997) PC and MAC versions available. Looks at earthquakes, hurricanes, tornadoes and duststorms as well as floods.

WEB SITES

For information on weather forecasts and predictions in the United Kingdom: http://www.meto.gov.uk

For information on flood warnings in the United Kingdom: http://www.environment-agency.gov.uk

For information on flood warnings and weather in the United States of America: http://www.state.me.us/mema/weather/flood.htm

For information on natural hazards including floods: www.ucl.ac.uk/geolsci/research/ben-grei/

For satellite images: http://www.earth.nasa.gov

Index

Page numbers in bold refer to illustrations.